MW01493655

Happy 10th Birthday

Made in the USA
San Bernardino, CA
20 March 2020

66024212R00068